COUNTRIES OF THE WORLD

Germany

Gareth Stevens Publishing
MILWAUKEE

About the Author: Richard Lord has lived in Germany for more than sixteen years. He is a free-lance writer and poet and has written several books on Germany.

PICTURE CREDITS

AKG Photo Berlin: 11 (both), 15 (bottom), 15 (center), 29 (bottom), 30 (top), 32, 45, 46, 74, 77 (bottom), 81, 82 (top), 83 (right)

A.N.A. Press Agency: Cover, 15 (top), 19, 54, 59, 84

Axiom Photographic Agency: 5, 7, 35

Susanna Burton: 1, 34

Gemeinde Oberammergau: 63

Dave G. Houser Stock Photography: 40, 42, 43, 78, 87, 91

Hutchison Library: 3 (center), 18, 44 (top), 58, 70

Inter Nationes: 10 (both), 13 (top), 16, 17 (right), 29 (top), 30 (bottom), 31, 33, 44 (bottom), 47, 56, 57, 60, 61, 64, 65, 66, 67, 71, 73 (both), 75, 76, 77 (top), 79, 82 (bottom), 83 (left), 85

International Photobank: 26, 62

Life File Photo Library: 21

Photobank Photolibrary/Singapore: 4, 38 (bottom), 51, 55

David Simson: 22, 24, 25, 28

Sylvia Cordaiy Photo Library: 89

Topham Picturepoint: 2, 3 (bottom), 6, 8 (bottom), 9, 12, 13 (bottom), 14, 17 (left), 20, 36 (both), 37, 39, 41, 50, 52, 53, 68, 72

Travel Ink: 3 (top), 8 (top), 38 (top)

Trip Photographic Library: 23, 27, 48, 49, 69, 80

Digital Scanning by Superskill Graphics Pte Ltd

Written by
RICHARD LORD

Edited by
ELLEN WHITE

Designed by
SHARIFAH FAUZIAH

Picture research by
SUSAN JANE MANUEL

First published in North America in 1999 by
Gareth Stevens Publishing
1555 North RiverCenter Drive, Suite 201
Milwaukee, Wisconsin 53212 USA

For a free color catalog describing
Gareth Stevens' list of high-quality books
and multimedia programs, call
1-800-542-2595 (USA) or
1-800-461-9120 (CANADA).
Gareth Stevens Publishing's
Fax: (414) 225-0377.
See our catalog, too, on the World Wide Web:
gsinc.com

© **TIMES EDITIONS PTE LTD 1999**
Originated and designed by
Times Books International
an imprint of Times Editions Pte Ltd
Times Centre, 1 New Industrial Road
Singapore 536196
http://www.timesone.com.sg/te

Library of Congress Cataloging-in-Publication Data
Lord, Richard.
Germany / Richard Lord.
p. cm. -- (Countries of the world)
Includes bibliographical references and index.
Summary: Introduces the geography, history, economy, natural resources, government, culture, and people of reunified Germany.
ISBN 0-8368-2261-7 (lib. bdg.)
1. Germany--Juvenile literature. [1. Germany.] I. Title.
II. Series: Countries of the world (Milwaukee, Wis.)
DD17.L67   1999
943--dc21   98-8859

Printed in Singapore

1 2 3 4 5 6 7 8 9 03 02 01 00 99

Contents

AN OVERVIEW OF GERMANY

Throughout its complex history, Germany has played an important role in Europe's development and culture. Bach and Beethoven are only two examples of Germany's contribution to classical music. German-born physicist Albert Einstein astonished the world with his general theory of relativity in the early twentieth century. German cars are prized for their elegance and power. Despite the nation's recent turbulent history and its division into West and East, modern, reunified Germany has emerged as a world leader in politics, economics, and culture.

Opposite: **Plaza in Munich. The building on the right is the City Hall, built in 1867. It is famous for its Glockenspiel with mechanical figures that perform twice a day in the summer.**

Below: **These children are having fun at a playground.**

THE FLAG OF GERMANY

This flag was used by Germany during several periods in its history, including the Weimar Republic (1919–1933). When Germany was divided into two countries in 1949, both East and West Germany adopted the same flag. The only difference was a communist emblem added in 1959 to the East German flag. Upon reunification in 1990, East and West Germany decided to keep the West's national name as well as its flag. The colors have been described by a German poet, writing at a turbulent time in his country's history, as: black for gunpowder, red for blood, and yellow as "the flame of golden glow."

Geography

Germany is the third largest country in the European Union, following France and Spain. It covers 137,744 square miles (357,000 square kilometers) of territory, which includes some of the most picturesque scenery and famous mountains and rivers in the world.

Germany is surrounded by nine other countries: Denmark to the north, the Netherlands, Belgium, Luxembourg, and France to the west, Switzerland and Austria to the south, and Poland and the Czech Republic to the east. The country still manages to have 1,018 miles (1,640 km) of coastline along the northern boundaries formed by the North Sea and the Baltic Sea.

A great many rivers flow through Germany. Historically, they were important in the development of commerce. Cities such as Hamburg, Dresden, and Frankfurt began as trading towns along important rivers. The largest and most famous river is the Rhine, which begins in the south, in the Swiss Alps, and flows 820 miles (1,319 km) northward into the North Sea. It is an important river,

Below: **The German Alps are along the border with Austria. They are divided from west to east into the Bavarian and the Berchtesgaden Alps. Zugspitze, at 9,718 feet (2,962 meters), is Germany's highest peak. Nearby is Garmisch-Partenkirchen, Germany's major ski resort and the largest town in the Bavarian Alps.**

Left: Canals wind their way throughout Hamburg, Germany's largest port. Located where the Alster, Bille, and Elbe rivers meet, and close to the North Sea, Hamburg has a long history as a trading center. It is also Germany's second largest city after Berlin. It boasts a rich cultural heritage and was the home of well-known classical composers Georg Friedrich Handel and Johannes Brahms.

both commercially as well as strategically. The Elbe is the second largest river. It is 724 miles (1,165 km) long and flows through the eastern part of the country. Other important rivers are the Main, the Oder, the Weser, and the Danube.

Northern Germany is relatively flat, with a broad plain extending to the sea. South and central Germany have a number of mountain ranges. In the center of the country are the Harz Mountains. The Bavarian Alps, in the south, form the largest and most impressive range. They are a continuation of the Swiss and Austrian Alps. Zugspitze, within the Bavarian Alps, reaches an elevation of 9,718 feet (2,962 m) and is Germany's highest peak.

Seasons

Germany has a temperate climate with four distinct seasons that, in most parts of the country, are neither too cold nor too hot. Along the northern coasts, the weather can get raw in late autumn and winter because of the strong, blustery winds. The high Alps in the south get the coolest weather. The mildest areas are in the southwest because of the sirocco, a warm wind that blows in from North Africa and the Mediterranean Sea.

Plants and Animals

Forests cover 30 percent of the country and are rich in needle-bearing and leaf-bearing trees — fir, spruce, pine, oak, birch, and beech. The Black Forest in southwestern Germany was named for the dark fir trees that make it look black and forbidding. Ever since the eighteenth century, the forest has attracted visitors who come to hike the many trails, look at the wildlife, and admire the scenery.

Flowers such as dog's mercury, sweet woodruff, and violets also thrive in the forests. Balsam, willow herb, monkshood, bilberry, foxglove, and wavy hair grass grow at higher altitudes.

Above: **Germany's famed Black Forest is a popular vacation spot.**

DYING FORESTS

Pollution is damaging trees and threatening Germany's beautiful forests. Countermeasures are being taken, but are they enough?
(A Closer Look, page 52)

Above: **Osprey and other animals and plants are protected in nature reserves.**

Germany has an astonishing diversity of animal life. Many of the animals, such as grouse, pheasants, buzzards, hawks, foxes, badgers, elk, and deer, are also found in North America. Large predators, such as the wolf and the lynx, are now very rare in Germany. Along with bears, these animals were once plentiful, and hunting was a popular sport. The German pronunciation of Berlin — "Bear-leen" — reflects the fact that this town was once the ruling prince's favorite bear-hunting preserve. Wild boar and deer are still hunted in Bavaria.

Commonly seen birds include sparrows, finches, jays, blackbirds, ravens, larks, thrushes, ducks, geese, swans, and along the coastal areas, seagulls. Rarer birds, such as sea eagles, cranes, storks, cormorants, bitterns, greylag geese, and osprey, live in the country's nature reserves.

Many territories along the former border between East and West Germany are now nature reserves. Because of restricted access to these areas for so many years, plants and animals remained undisturbed and, therefore, flourished. A national park along the border with the Czech Republic is also a nature reserve.

Opposite: **Located in Bavaria, this house is surrounded by natural beauty. During the warm, summer months, the countryside is filled with flowers in bloom.**

History

The traditional starting point of German history is A.D. 9, when Arminius, a Germanic chieftain, halted the expansion of the Roman Empire at the Rhine and Danube rivers. Until A.D. 350, Germanic tribes, such as the Ostrogoths, Visigoths, and Vandals, co-existed with the Roman Empire despite military conflicts among themselves and with the Romans. As the Roman Empire weakened, however, these tribes formed independent Germanic kingdoms within Roman territory. In 476, the ailing western Roman Empire finally collapsed. Under King Clovis, the Franks, one of the Germanic tribes, emerged dominant. They converted to Christianity during his reign, and, by the beginning of the eighth century, had conquered a large part of Western Europe.

Above: **Charlemagne, known in Germany as Karl der Grosse, standardized the laws in his empire and introduced Latin as the official language.**

An Expanding Empire

Charlemagne, known in Germany as Karl der Grosse, was king of the Franks from 768 to 814. He greatly expanded the Frankish empire, and conquered tribes were converted to Christianity. He was given the title of Holy Roman Emperor in 800 by the pope in Rome, a title German kings continued to bear until 1806.

After Charlemagne's death, the vast Frankish kingdom was divided among his sons. The eastern portion was eventually ruled by a grandson of Charlemagne, Ludwig the German. The Frankish empire acquired administrative control over the Roman Catholic Church in the tenth century, after a series of military campaigns in northern Italy.

The empire continued to expand over the next three hundred years. This period saw frequent conflicts among German princes and confrontations with the increasingly powerful Roman Catholic Church. In the thirteenth century, the Hapsburg family gained dominance and continued to be the ruling dynasty for the next few centuries.

Above: **Martin Luther's defiance of the Roman Catholic Church sparked the Protestant Reformation. His success was partly due to developments in science and technology that changed the way people interpreted the world.**

The Protestant Reformation and the Thirty Years' War

In 1517, Martin Luther, a German monk, boldly challenged the authority of the Roman Catholic Church. He denounced the authority of the pope and the special status of the clergy, posting

his statements on the church door at Wittenberg to protest these and other abuses in the Catholic Church. A peasant rebellion against the Church broke out in 1525 and was put down a year later. However, Christianity in Germany split permanently into opposing groups of Catholics and Protestants. Internal struggles continued into the seventeenth century, and much of the power of the emperors, gained during the Hapsburg dynasty, was lost during the Thirty Years' War (1618–1648). Germany then became a collection of small kingdoms governed by various rulers fighting for power.

The German Reich

The last Holy Roman emperor, Franz II, left the throne in 1806 when parts of Germany were occupied by the French during the Napoleonic Wars. When the wars ended in 1815, a German Confederation was formed, but the long-awaited unification of Germany did not take place until 1871. Under the leadership of Otto von Bismarck, prime minister of Prussia (the largest and most powerful German state), the German Empire, or *Reich* (RIKE), was born. During the next few decades, the new nation witnessed amazing achievements. By 1900, Germany was the second largest industrial power after the United States.

Above, left: **Otto von Bismarck began his career as a diplomat. When he became head of the Prussian government in 1862, one of his first steps was to modernize the army. His leadership helped create the German Empire. As chancellor, he was also largely responsible for the empire's success.**

Above, right: **The German Empire was formed on January 18, 1871, and King William I of Prussia was made *Kaiser* (KYE-zer), the German word for emperor. The empire consisted of twenty states and three cities and lasted for forty-seven years.**

World War I

With its expanding political powers, Germany often came into conflict with other European powers. In 1914, war broke out and did not end until 1918, with a humiliating defeat for Germany and its allies. The end of the war also meant the end of the empire. The Kaiser was forced to resign, and the first republic was set up — the Weimar Republic, with a constitution and elected leaders.

Although well-intentioned, the new government was unable to deal with the problems of post-war Germany, followed by the worldwide depression of the 1930s. The country's social and economic ills paved the way for Adolf Hitler and his National Socialist Party, or Nazis, to seize power in 1933.

The Nazis and World War II

Nazi Germany pursued an aggressive foreign policy by reclaiming territory lost as a result of the Versailles Treaty that ended World War I. At first, world leaders did not want to confront a newly powerful Germany. However, Great Britain and France declared war in 1939 when German troops marched into Poland. The United States entered the war in 1941.

Above: **Brandenburg Sachsenhausen Concentration Camp is a grim reminder of vicious hate campaigns that the Nazis launched against groups of people, particularly Jews. Innocent people were rounded up in concentration camps, where an estimated six million of them died.**

Opposite: **Located in the middle of East Germany, Berlin, the former capital, was also divided after World War II. West Berlin became part of West Germany. The Berlin Wall was built by East Germany in August 1961 to stop the flow of refugees into West Berlin.**

The German army scored a series of shockingly quick military victories at first. However, the country's people and resources were badly overextended and unable to withstand the combined military strength of its foes. Germany surrendered on May 8, 1945. Defeat brought about the collapse of the Nazi government and the close of the darkest chapter in German history.

Two Germanys

After the war, Germany ceased to exist as a united country. For four years it was occupied and ruled by military councils representing the world's four Allied powers — the United States, Great Britain, France, and the Union of Soviet Socialist Republics (U.S.S.R.). The zones occupied by Great Britain, France, and the United States increasingly clashed with the Soviet-held zone, resulting in a split. In 1949, the Federal Republic of Germany was formed, with a democratically elected government. It was known as West Germany. In the same year, the German Democratic Republic was established as a satellite of the U.S.S.R. and was referred to as East Germany. This division lasted thirty-five years.

THE BERLIN AIRLIFT

The monument above was built to honor those who broke the Soviet-imposed Berlin blockade in 1948 by flying supplies into the beleaguered city.
(A Closer Look, page 44)

The Economic Miracle

Both countries recovered quickly from the war. By the 1960s, West Germany was the world's third largest economy. East Germany was the economic engine for Europe's communist countries.

Although the two Germanys shared the same history, language, and culture, conflicts between them grew. The 855-mile (1,375-km) border known as the Iron Curtain was fortified, and the Berlin Wall was constructed in 1961 to prevent defections.

Reunification

The collapse of communism in Europe in 1989 made it possible for thousands of East Germans to travel to West Germany. Those who stayed behind began demonstrating for more rights and reforms. The Berlin Wall was opened, and in March 1990, East Germans voted for reunification with West Germany.

On October 3, 1990, the two countries officially merged. Elections for a united Germany were held in December, and Helmut Kohl was elected chancellor.

Below: **A treaty of reunification became official on October 3, 1990 and was cause for many celebrations, including this one at the Reichstag, the parliament building in Berlin.**

Louis II (1845–1886)

Nicknamed Mad King Ludwig, Louis II was the king of Bavaria from 1864 to 1886. A German patriot, he chose to join Prussia against France in the war of 1870–71. In response to urging from Bismarck, Louis wrote a letter to Germany's princes encouraging them to form a German empire. In return, special privileges were granted to Bavaria, including money for building castles.

Louis II increasingly withdrew from politics and became a patron of the arts. His most fantastic castle, Neuschwanstein, was decorated with scenes from Richard Wagner's operas. In 1886, he was declared insane by a panel of doctors and later found drowned in a lake near one of his castles.

Louis II

Adolf Hitler (1889–1945)

Born in Austria, Adolf Hitler was a frustrated artist when he moved to Munich in 1913. He became leader of the National Socialist Party and was jailed after a failed coup in 1923. During that time, he wrote *Mein Kampf*, a book expressing his disregard for democratic government and his hatred of the Jews. After becoming chancellor in 1933, Hitler adopted the title *Führer* (FYUR-er), or leader. He established a totalitarian state. His aggressive foreign policies resulted in World War II. When it became evident that Germany could no longer withstand the military onslaught of its enemies, Hitler committed suicide in his bunker outside Berlin in 1945.

Adolf Hitler

Konrad Adenauer (1876–1967)

As the first chancellor of the Federal Republic of Germany (West Germany), Konrad Adenauer watched over the country's reconstruction after World War II. Born in Cologne, he studied law and entered politics in 1906. Under the Nazis, he was stripped of his political posts and sent to a concentration camp. After the war, he helped form a new political party, the Christian Democratic Union (CDU). When he became chancellor in 1949, Adenauer worked to forge friendly ties with Germany's former enemies and helped the country regain its importance in Europe.

Konrad Adenauer

Government and the Economy

Present-day Germany is a democratic republic. All German citizens aged eighteen or over have the right to vote in local, state, and national elections. The German parliament is composed of two houses. The *Bundestag* (boon-des-TAHG) is made up of 672 elected representatives, many of whom win their seats through the "party vote." The *Bundesrat* (boon-des-RAHT) consists of legislators from individual states who are appointed by their state government.

Political Parties

Under the party vote system, each voter is given two votes. The first is for a specific candidate for a specific office. The second vote is for a particular political party. Half of the parliament seats are distributed to party members according to the percentage of the vote their political party received.

WOMEN IN GOVERNMENT

Women have been fighting hard to get better representation in the government. Their numbers in the Bundestag have slowly increased over the years but are still far from reaching equal numbers with men.
(A Closer Look, page 72)

Below: **A voter turns in her ballot.**

The Christian Democratic Union (CDU) and its affiliate, the Christian Social Union (CSU), support free enterprise. The Social Democratic Party (SDP) promotes a strong central government and social welfare programs. The Green Party campaigns on environmental issues. Since the Green Party won its first seats in the Bundestag in 1983, environmental protection has gained increasing political importance.

Above, left: **Claudia Nolte was appointed in 1994 as head of the Ministry for Family, Senior Citizens, Women, and Youth. At twenty-eight, she was the youngest minister to be appointed to the newly formed German federal government.**

State Parliaments

There are sixteen German states, including three city-states — Berlin, Hamburg, and Bremen. Each state has a democratically elected parliament. The two-vote system also applies to local elections, although mayors are sometimes elected by popular vote.

Above, right: **As chancellor of West Germany, Helmut Kohl oversaw Germany's reunification and became the country's first chancellor in 1990. In September, 1998, Gerhard Schroeder, of the Social Democratic Party, replaced Kohl as chancellor.**

The Chancellor and the President

The government's executive power is divided into two positions — the chancellor and the president. As the leader of the Bundestag's most powerful political party, the chancellor exercises supreme power in Germany. The president is elected by a special body of Bundestag and Bundesrat members. As head of state, the president's role is more ceremonial than the chancellor's.

Economy

Germany's economy is the third largest in the world, a position it has held for almost thirty years. With few natural resources, Germany relies heavily on exports of products from key industries, including cars, electronics, pharmaceutical products, and food items. A liberal trade policy has helped promote foreign trade, especially within the European community.

As a leading world power, Germany has major banks whose decisions affect European and international finances. The Deutsche mark is a yardstick for measuring the value of other currencies, including the U.S. dollar. Soon, along with some other European countries, Germany will switch to the Euro, the new EU currency.

Transportation

Germany enjoys one of the world's best transportation systems. Of the country's thirteen airports, Frankfurt is Europe's biggest and busiest. The country's railroad system is a model of efficiency, and trains travel to all parts of the country with amazing punctuality. Rivers have always been important to the development of German trade. The largest and most famous is the Rhine. Local

Below: **About one-third of the work force is employed in the manufacturing sector. Most heavy industry, like this steel mill, is located in the Ruhr Valley, the region where German industrialization began in the early 1800s.**

Left: Cruising Germany's scenic rivers is a popular pastime. The rivers also remain important arteries of trade.

transportation, including street cars, buses, subways, and suburban trains, is fast and convenient. The German road system sets a standard for many other countries, especially its network of highways known as the *Autobahn* (AW-to-bahn).

Work

Germans are a hard-working people, but they have a short working year, with five to six weeks of paid vacation and many public holidays. Although once a clear majority, the number of workers in heavy industry today stands at just 38 percent. Workers' councils give employees a say in management. There are seventeen labor unions in Germany. Office workers make up about 59 percent of the work force. Civil servants are another significant group at 7.7 percent of the work force.

RECYCLING

Germans concern for their environment is seen in their support of recycling trash. The most popular system is the Green Dot system, which relies on cooperation between manufacturers and consumers.

(A Closer Look, page 66)

SUPERHIGHWAYS

Originally built for military vehicles, the network of superhighways, or Autobahn, is well suited to Germany's high-performance cars.

(A Closer Look, page 68)

People and Lifestyle

Germany is about the size of Montana, but its population is one-third that of the United States. Although most Germans originated from neighboring regions within Western Europe, they have varied cultural traditions and lifestyles.

Regional Differences

Germans are proud of their regional identities, often thinking of themselves first as Bavarians, Swabians, Saxons, East Friesians, or Hessians, and second as Germans. One reason is that Germany was once many different tiny kingdoms, which were not unified until 1871. Until recently, few Germans moved

THE MAX PLANCK SOCIETY

What is the "super nose?" — just one of many achievements by German scientists who are part of the Max Planck Society.
(*A Closer Look, page 60*)

Left: Regional costumes, such as the Bavarian clothes worn by these children, are now used mostly for special occasions.

out of their hometown; most people tended to stay in the area where they were born.

Some of the regional differences are physical. People in the south tend to be darker and shorter than northerners, who are usually tall, blond, and blue-eyed. In spoken German, regional accents can be very pronounced. There are also differences in dress. If you want to see the classic image of a German man dressed in short leather pants called *Lederhose* (LAY-dare-HOSE-uh), the Janker jacket, and the peaked hunter's cap, your best chance is in Bavaria. This is also where you will find women wearing *Dirndl* (DURN-dil) skirts and ruffled shirts resembling those of Heidi, heroine of the popular children's story. Germans claim that people in the north are quiet and tight-lipped, whereas Bavarians are the most fun-loving, but these are, of course, only broad generalizations.

Below: **When the German "economic miracle" took off in the 1950s, there was a shortage of workers. Many were recruited from other countries by German companies. Today, the largest groups of foreigners are Turks, Italians, Greeks, Spaniards, Moroccans, and citizens of the former Yugoslavia.**

Foreign Population

Immigrants from other parts of Europe and from Asia form large communities in Germany. Although many of them were born and raised in Germany, they are still considered foreigners. Over seven million people (almost 9 percent of the country's population) are considered foreigners rather than Germans. The foreign population is unevenly distributed around the country, but Frankfurt has the greatest number.

Family Life

For the most part, family life in Germany resembles that in most Western countries. The nuclear family — both parents and children — is the basic family unit. In urban areas, both parents usually work to keep up with expenses.

German families tend to be small, with one or two children. Large extended families are rare but can still be found in rural areas of southern Germany. Many non-foreign married couples in Germany today are childless. Some demographers are worried that the country's birth rate is barely keeping up with the death rate. Only foreign residents of Germany have enough children in their families to sustain the population.

Traveling is a favorite German pastime. Prosperity and favorable exchange rates have made Germany a nation of globe-trotters. Holidays are often celebrated with short trips abroad, either to countries within Europe or farther afield.

KINDERGARTENS

The first kindergarten in the world was established in Germany in 1837. Its purpose was to expose children between the ages of three and six to new sensory experiences. With so many women working today, kindergartens have become an important institution in modern-day Germany.
(A Closer Look, page 56)

PRIVATE GARDENS

Private gardens for city dwellers are grouped together in special sections of town. These gardens are for planting flowers and vegetables. They also serve as retreats from the stresses of urban life.
(A Closer Look, page 64)

Left: House pets are loved and well cared for in Germany.

Opposite: Christmas Eve features a big family celebration. The Christmas tree is decorated, and gifts are exchanged.

Educational System

In the first four years of school in Germany, all pupils study together. The process of "streaming" starts in the fifth grade. Streaming involves putting children into three kinds of schools depending on their abilities.

The *Hauptschule* (HOWPT-shool-uh) prepares students for jobs in trade and industry; the *Realschule* (ray-AHL-shool-uh) provides a broader education, appropriate for middle-level postings in business or public service jobs; the *Gymnasium* (gim-NAH-zee-oom) is the academically select school, which readies students for university studies and executive positions in industry and commerce. Furthermore, students who attend Gymnasium have thirteen years of schooling rather than twelve. At the end of their studies, they take a battery of difficult tests, called *das Abitur* (dahs ah-bee-TOOR), for admission to universities or jobs in government or the private sector.

Students in Germany go to school for only half a day and leave at around noon. Substitute teachers are rarely used, so students are often sent home early if a teacher is not available.

Below: German children's career paths are determined in the fifth grade when they are tested and put in one of three schools preparing them for jobs in industry, public service, or executive-level positions.

German schools do not offer their students much in the way of extracurricular activities. This reflects an educational philosophy that emphasizes teaching academic or trade skills rather than sports and hobbies. Special interests are left to families, church and community organizations, and various clubs to pursue.

Everyone is required to attend school for at least nine years and up to thirteen years if they are in Gymnasium schools. Each state runs its own schools. About 95 percent of children attend state schools; the rest go to private schools. These are usually run by churches or are the Waldorf schools created for less competitive children.

One in four children receives a college education. Today's university students enjoy a great deal of freedom and are given a say in how universities are run. It has not always been that way. A century ago, in Heidelberg and at other universities, there was a jail for students found guilty of bad behavior!

Since reunification, schools in former East Germany are changing their educational system. They no longer teach communist ideas and philosophy. Russian used to be the main foreign language taught, but now it is English.

Above: **German students attend particular schools not on the basis of where they live but how well they perform academically.**

LEARNING A TRADE

Young people who want to learn a trade work under the guidance of a master craftsman. Upon completion of the training program, apprentices are awarded a certificate that entitles them to work their trade at full pay.

(A Closer Look, page 58)

Religion

Freedom of religion is strongly anchored in the German constitution, a guarantee that the discriminatory policies of the Nazis will never be repeated.

Religious life in Germany is dominated by the Lutheran Church with 28.2 million members, and the Roman Catholic Church with 27.9 million. There is no strict separation of church and state as there is in North America. The churches receive money from the government in the form of a church tax collected

Left: **St. Stephen's Church in Mainz. The beautiful stained glass windows were designed by the artist Marc Chagall.**

from registered church members. Religious instruction is allowed in public schools and is a required course in most areas. Sunday is a day of rest when most shops and businesses are closed.

However, the two churches do not exercise the influence their size and position might suggest. One reason is that most church members attend church only for important ceremonies and occasions. Just over 5 percent of German Lutherans are regular churchgoers. Among Catholics, the figure is 19 percent. Still, many people in Germany appreciate the good work churches do,

particularly in helping the needy, and they remain official taxpaying members.

Above: **Over two million Muslims live in Germany. The majority are Turkish.**

In recent years, other religions have gained importance as the number of foreigners practicing other faiths has increased. Probably the most significant of these in terms of numbers and influence is Islam. Today, there are an estimated 2.6 million Muslims in Germany. Other significant religions include the Christian Orthodox Church, the Methodist Church, the Baptist Church, and Judaism. These smaller religious groups tend to be very observant of their religion and are slowly changing Germany's religious profile.

Language and Literature

Did you know that English belongs to the Germanic family of languages? English was once a German dialect that developed into a different language over time. Many similarities still exist between the two languages, but the differences are what surprise English speakers most.

Differences in pronunciation provide some good examples. The word *situation* is spelled the same in both languages. However, in German it is pronounced, "zi-too-WAT-tzee-OHN." "W" in German is pronounced like an English "V," while the German "V" is pronounced like the English "F." This means that *Volkswagen,* the name of a popular German car, is pronounced "Folks-vah-gen" in German.

The German language also has a sign called the umlaut — two dots written above the vowels A, O, and U. The umlaut changes a word's pronunciation. For instance, *Sohn*, the German word for "son," is pronounced "zoan." The plural form, *Söhne*, has an umlaut and is pronounced "Zurr-nuh."

Literature

Germany has a rich and long history of literary achievement, beginning with the sagas of the great heroes and gods of German legends. The oldest text was written in the early 800s and is the story of the hero, Hildebrand. The *Nibelungenlied* is another epic poem, written in the thirteenth century by an unknown poet.

One of Martin Luther's greatest achievements in the early fifteenth century was translating the Bible into German. The printing press was developed at about the same time, and written German became widely used.

German Classicism in the late eighteenth century produced two of Germany's greatest writers — Friedrich Schiller and Johann Wolfgang von Goethe. Goethe is famous for his masterpiece, *Faust*, the story of a man who sells his soul to the devil for universal knowledge.

The early nineteenth century was the height of German Romanticism, led by the poet Heinrich Heine. It was also a period when writers such as the Brothers Grimm recovered the nearly lost treasures of old German songs and fairy tales.

Below: The English and German languages share many striking similarities.

The three major German writers of the first half of the twentieth century were very different in style and temperament. Nobel Prize winner Thomas Mann was a conservative, philosophical writer with classical tastes. He wrote long novels with extremely long sentences. Bertolt Brecht was a devout Marxist, whose experimental plays, stories, and poems explored the problems of the working class. Hermann Hesse was a mystic who introduced Eastern ideas to German literature.

Heinrich Böll (1917–1985) and Günter Grass (b. 1927) have both written extensively about the German experience during the Nazi rise to power, World War II, and its aftermath. Böll won the Nobel Prize for Literature in 1972. He died in 1985.

Above: The Tin Drum, written by German author Günter Grass, was made into an Academy Award-winning film in 1980. This novel, like many works by Grass, deals with the traumas Germans suffered during World War II.

THE BROTHERS GRIMM

"Hansel and Gretel" is one of many well-known fairy tales written down by the Brothers Grimm in the nineteenth century.

(A Closer Look, page 46)

Arts

Germans often refer to themselves as a *Kulturvolk* (kool-TOOR-fulk), a people of culture — an indication of the high value they place on the arts.

Music

Probably the art form most closely identified with Germany is music because many of the world's most famous composers are German. Bach, Beethoven, Brahms, and Handel are known for their classical compositions. Richard Strauss and Kurt Weill composed in the twentieth century. Weill wrote *The Threepenny Opera,* which opens with the well-known song, "Mack the Knife."

Germans' passion for music is seen in the public support it receives. There are 195 orchestras and 95 government-subsidized opera houses and concert halls. Young people are encouraged to develop their musical talents in special programs at school and at home. In addition to producing professional musicians, Germany has many amateur musical groups.

Above: **Ludwig van Beethoven (1770–1827) was born in Bonn. He is famous for his emotionally rich symphonies.**

Left: **Germans love music and encourage young people to develop their musical abilities. In addition to school music programs, many amateur performing groups also exist.**

Left: This painting was done by Joseph Beuys (1921–1986), perhaps post-war Germany's best known artist. Museums throughout the world show his avant-garde work — paintings and sculptures that transformed commonly used materials and objects into art.

Painting and Sculpture

During the Middle Ages, artists were anonymous because the art they produced was displayed in churches in the form of altars, stained-glass windows, and religious wall paintings.

The Italian Renaissance, along with the Protestant Reformation, reached Germany in the late fifteenth and early sixteenth centuries. A double emphasis on art and individual achievement produced Germany's first fully recognized artists. The giants of this period were Albrecht Dürer, Lucas Cranach the Elder, Hans Holbein the Younger, and Hans Baldung.

German art of the twentieth century is a reflection of the destruction and loss of two world wars, as well as a search for the new and different. Joseph Beuys is known for his paintings, collages, and sculptures using discarded metal and other common materials.

Today, there are 1,500 museums and art galleries in Germany. About 86 percent receive government funding and support from corporate sponsors. Art is prominently displayed in public spaces for everyone to enjoy.

GOVERNMENT FUNDING OF THE ARTS

German artists formerly relied on sponsors who were usually wealthy noblemen. Now they receive financial support from the government. As a result, Germany has maintained its strong cultural tradition and prominence as an artistic center.
(*A Closer Look,* page 54)

TECHNO MUSIC

Although known for its classical musical traditions, Germany is also at the forefront of popular music. Techno music is a mixture of synthesized sounds, with a beat that is perfect for disco dancing.
(*A Closer Look,* page 70)

Architecture

Churches were the earliest artistic achievements in Germany, beginning with the Romanesque cathedrals built in the late ninth century. The Gothic period, from the thirteenth to the fifteenth century, produced such classics as the majestic Cologne Cathedral. In the mid-seventeenth century, stunning castles were built in the Baroque style. Charlottenburg Palace in Berlin, built for the Prussian King Frederick the Great, is one of the most impressive buildings of that era.

The twentieth century saw an emphasis on bringing good architectural design to utilitarian structures, such as factories and company headquarters. The administration building of the Höchst chemical plant, built in 1925, was designed by the great architect Peter Behrens.

Probably the most enduring modern architectural influence has been the Bauhaus movement that began in 1919. It was founded by architects such as Walter Gropius and Mies van der Rohe who wanted to create better living environments for Germany's workers. The architects incorporated new social ideas into their designs.

Most of the buildings built after World War II were purely functional. Germany was in ashes and rubble, and the impulse was to rebuild as quickly as possible. In the last forty years, foreign architects have gained prominence. Britain's Sir Norman Foster is re-doing the Reichstag building, home of the German Bundestag.

CASTLES

Germany is a land of many castles. This is because the country used to be a patchwork of tiny kingdoms. As a symbol of authority, each ruler had his own castle. Many castles were built in ornate and fanciful architectural styles.
(A Closer Look, page 50)

Left: Designed by architect Walter Gropius, this office building with its simple lines and functional look is typical of Bauhaus architecture. Rather than create individual works for the wealthy, architects of the Bauhaus school designed for the masses.

Left: Marlene Dietrich was one of many famous film stars to leave Germany in the 1930s and go to Hollywood. As the Nazis rose to power, many artists feared persecution and fled to other countries.

Theater

In the Roaring Twenties, the theaters of Berlin were considered some of the most exciting in the world. Among the leading figures of this period were the playwright Bertolt Brecht, composers Kurt Weill and Hanns Eisler, and directors Max Reinhardt and Erwin Piscator. Many of these artists were forced to emigrate when the Nazis came to power, and some of them settled in the United States.

THE OBERAMMERGAU PASSION PLAY

The Oberammergau Passion Play is one of the longest-running amateur theatrical events. This reenactment of the life and death of Jesus Christ began in the early seventeenth century. It is performed by the townspeople every ten years.

(*A Closer Look, page 62*)

Leisure and Festivals

Germany has the reputation of being a nation of workaholics, but nothing could be farther from the truth. In fact, Germans work almost three hundred hours a year less than Americans. So what do they do with all their free time?

Clubs

The German people have a fascination with joining clubs. In this relatively small country, there are over three hundred thousand officially registered clubs. These clubs are called *Vereine* (fur-INE-nuh) in German and are formed to pursue just about any activity, from stamp collecting to playing skat, a popular but complex card game. Clubs also exist for people who breed dogs, want to practice a foreign language, or are bicycling enthusiasts.

German schools do not usually have sports teams. So the only way for students to get involved in a sport is to join a sports club. These clubs form teams that play against each other in competitions. People of all ages are attracted to sports clubs, and one in three Germans is a member of a sports club.

Above: **Making floats for a street parade is another activity usually done through clubs.**

The Beautiful Outdoors

Whether winter or summer, Germans enjoy spending time in their beautiful forests and mountains. Hiking, rock climbing, and walking are popular pastimes. The Alps have many well-marked trails that draw amateur walkers, adventurous mountaineers, or students on school trips. In the winter, skiing and skating are popular.

WANDERLUST

Travel anywhere in the world and you will probably meet some Germans along the way. They are the world's greatest tourists, with a passion for seeing the world. Many travel to nearby countries, such as Austria, Italy, Greece, and France, but others go farther afield to Asia, Africa, and North America.

Left: Sports activities are arranged by clubs rather than by schools. These boys are in a soccer club. Soccer is Germany's most popular sport.

Sports

Soccer, or *Fussball* (FOOS-ball), is by far the most popular spectator and team sport in Germany. The former West German team won the World Cup three times — in 1954, 1974, and 1990. Amateur teams are organized by clubs. The National League has eighteen teams plus a lower division with twenty teams. At the end of the season, the two top teams of the lower division trade places with the bottom two of the National League.

German athletes excel in other sports as well. Katarina Witt won Olympic gold medals in 1984 and 1988 for ice skating. Swimmer Franziska von Almsick won four medals at the 1992 Olympics. In cycling, twenty-three-year-old Jan Ullrich became the first German to win the Tour de France in 1997. Tennis stars, such as Boris Becker and Steffi Graf, have inspired more people to take up the sport, and new tennis clubs have been springing up. Becker won the Wimbledon singles title in 1985 when he was seventeen. In 1988, at the age of nineteen, Graf won the Golden Grand Slam — all four of the major international tennis competitions plus the Olympic gold medal.

Opposite: Germany's Jurgen Klinsmann celebrates his second goal against the Russian soccer team at the Euro '96 Championship game.

Below, left: Boris Becker began playing professional tennis when he was fifteen. At seventeen, he won the Wimbledon singles title.

Below, right: For about ten years, Steffi Graf dominated women's tennis. She was at her peak in 1988 when she won the Grand Slam.

Festivals

Germany has so many festivals that it seems just as one is winding down, another is starting. Some have a Christian focus, but many festivals date back to ancient times.

The biggest festival is Carnival, or *Karneval* (KAHR-neh-vahl). It is usually held in February and marks the beginning of the Catholic fasting month, Lent. Christmas is celebrated on December 25 and 26, which are public holidays. Christmas merriment begins long before in the markets set up on city streets. People walk around eating, drinking, shopping, and getting into the holiday spirit.

Above: Carnival costumes are often very elaborate and prepared months in advance.

CARNIVAL

Germany's biggest festival began during pagan times. It is a religious festival marking the beginning of Lent, the Christian fasting month.

(A Closer Look, page 48)

Left: Munich's Oktoberfest at night.

Good Harvests

Many festivals celebrate important events in Germany's farming communities. In northern Germany, for example, there are processions of horse-riders. Shepherds' Run in Stuttgart features a foot race. The winner is declared King of the Shepherds. November is a time for festivals in the Rhineland, where grapes are grown. The world-famous beer festival, Oktoberfest, is held in early October in the brewing capital of Munich. Originally a wedding celebration for a prince of Bavaria, the event was so popular that it grew into a state agricultural fair, now held every year.

Left: Traditional dances performed at a festival in southern Germany.

Festivals have been revived in some areas not only to preserve the local heritage but also to attract tourists. These celebrations include street processions, open-air dancing, and stalls selling traditional handicrafts. Every year, the town of Hameln (Hamelin) reenacts the legend of the Pied Piper. An annual ten-day shooting festival in Hannover attracts over five thousand entrants.

October 3 is a non-religious holiday and celebrates Germany's reunification in 1990. Labor Day is celebrated on May 1. Clubs also sponsor annual festivals and competitions.

Food

Germans love to eat and are famous for their delicious foods. They are not in the habit of eating between-meal snacks. Instead, they have additional meals — a "second breakfast" and afternoon coffee and cakes. The second breakfast is eaten mid-morning and usually consists of a roll or pretzel accompanied by coffee or tea.

The main meal is eaten in the middle of the day and often has three full courses. People eat a simple supper in the evening — bread, cheese, cold cuts, and perhaps a salad.

Kaffee

Der Kaffee (kahf-FAY), which means "coffee," is served in the late afternoon and includes cakes, along with coffee or tea. The offerings for a typical Kaffee can be a simple roll studded with raisins or more elaborate creations, such as a Black Forest cherry cake with plenty of whipped cream. Instead of coffee, children drink hot chocolate or fruit juices.

Below: **German baked goods range from elegant pastries to oversized pretzels, such as these.**

Left: As the name suggests, frankfurters, or hot dogs, originated in the city of Frankfurt. Sauerkraut is pickled cabbage, a popular German side dish.

Dining Etiquette

Before they begin eating, Germans wish each other *"Guten Appetit"* (GOO-ten upp-eh-TEET), meaning "Enjoy your meal." In restaurants and cafés, strangers often sit together. But very rarely do they talk to each other except to say "Guten appetit" when the food is served and *"Auf Wiedersehen"* (owff VEE-dair-SAY-hen), or "good-bye," when the meal is over.

Favorite Foods

Traditionally, the favorite German meat is pork. There is an old saying that in Germany a cook uses every part of the pig except the "oink!" For example, *Schnitzel* (SHNIT-tsuhl) is a thin, breaded pork cutlet. One of the most famous German meat preparations is the German *Wurst* (VORST), or sausage. Wursts are usually made with pork, but other meats are used, too. Potatoes are popular, as are dumplings and noodles. A favorite method for preserving cabbage in winter is to pound it and set it in salt to make *Sauerkraut* (ZAUER-kraut). A German dessert enjoyed throughout the world is apple strudel, a pastry made with apples, raisins, and ground almonds.

A CLOSER LOOK AT GERMANY

This section takes you beyond the surface for a more in-depth look at Germany. The following topics offer glimpses of important moments in German history, key aspects of German culture, and insights on issues important to modern-day Germany.

Reunification in 1990 began a new chapter in German history that is still unfolding. Although the country was divided after World War II, it must not be forgotten that Germany first became a nation only in 1871. With each unification, there have been problems to solve. This time, the challenge is creating a national and economic identity that is compatible with citizens from both East and West Germany.

Germany has made important contributions to the arts, science, and technology. Once home to leading classical composers, such as Bach and Beethoven, the country is now in the forefront of modern pop music, with the electronic sounds of techno music. The Max Planck Society is a renowned organization of scientific institutes. A pioneering German came up with the idea of kindergartens to help children's early development. And almost everyone has read the Grimms' fairy tales, which were first written down by two German brothers.

Above: **A plaza in Frankfurt. Modern Germany has retained its Old World charm.**

Opposite: **Outdoor cafés such as this one in Berlin are a common sight. They are ideal places to go for something to eat and drink, as well as to visit with friends and relax.**

The Berlin Airlift

At the end of World War II, a thoroughly defeated Germany was divided into four occupation zones administered by the major powers that had fought and won the war against Nazi Germany — the United States, Britain, France, and the Soviet Union. In addition, the capital city of Berlin was divided into four zones and also occupied.

Conflicts arose among the occupying nations as to the economic and political direction Germany should take. The zone occupied by the Soviet Union was looking more and more like a communist-run system. The three other zones became increasingly democratic and open to a free market system.

The old currency, however, was virtually worthless. Most business was conducted using the barter system, which called for the exchange of goods rather than money. In order for Germany to develop a modern economy, a new currency was needed. Tensions came to a head in June 1948 when the leaders of the three Western-occupied zones introduced a new currency, the Deutsche mark.

The Soviets realized that accepting the new currency would mean accepting the free market system. This would put an end to their plans to dominate the eastern areas. So they rejected the Deutsche mark and decided to keep it out of West Berlin by

Above: **The Berlin Wall became a symbol of communist oppression. With the fall of the East German government in 1989, joyful citizens from the East and West tore the wall down.**

Left: **In defiance of the Soviet blockade of West Berlin, Allied planes that had once dropped bombs on Germany flew in food and much needed supplies to the besieged city.**

cutting the city off from the rest of Germany. Since Berlin was surrounded by the Soviet-held zone, this was easy. All roads and railway lines running into West Berlin were blockaded.

Soviet leader Josef Stalin and his advisers believed that West Berlin, cut off from food, fuel, and medical supplies, would capitulate and become part of the Soviet-occupied zone. However, they had not counted on the resolve of the Western Allies and the heroic resilience of the West Berliners who were determined not to fall under communist domination.

The Berlin blockade began on June 24, 1948. Within a few days, the Western Allies, using mostly American planes, began flying supplies into the city. In those days, air transportation was not as common as it is today. The planes used for this mission were mostly military aircraft that had been used in combat just a few years earlier to defeat Germany.

Finally, on May 4, 1949, the Soviet-led blockade ended. While it lasted, 279,114 flights delivered 2.34 million tons of goods to the beleaguered city. A monument was built to honor the heroism of those who resisted the economic stranglehold, thus ensuring West Berlin's existence as a separate and democratic entity.

The Brothers Grimm

"Snow White," "Little Red Riding Hood," "Cinderella," and "Hansel and Gretel" are famous fairy tales of German origin. The stories have been told for many centuries. However, they were not written down until the nineteenth century. Today, they are known as Grimm's Fairy Tales because they were first written down by two brothers, Jacob and Wilhelm Grimm.

The Brothers Grimm were born in the late eighteenth century in Hanau, east of Frankfurt. They studied law, but their love of German folklore prompted them to take up careers in literary research instead.

At the time, Germany was not a country but a patchwork of small scattered states and kingdoms. A united Germany was only an ideal shared by artists and intellectuals. These people worked hard to a create a national literature that would inspire others to come together to create a German nation.

The Brothers Grimm saw that one way of achieving this end was to collect the fairy tales and sagas that had been told by German-speaking people over the centuries. Their collection of children's nursery rhymes and fairy tales was published in 1812, and a book of German sagas came out three years later.

The brothers made a good team. Jacob was a researcher and scholar who recovered most of the old stories by listening to people tell them and by locating nearly lost and forgotten antiquated texts. Jacob's writing style was somewhat dull, however. Wilhelm, on the other hand, was a skilled storyteller. It was Wilhelm's literary abilities that turned his brother's research into stories that have engaged the imagination of children and adults around the world ever since.

The Brothers Grimm went on to do other studies of German language and culture. Their works set a standard for a new kind of research — the study of folklore. In 1840, the brothers were invited by the Prussian king to lecture at the university in Berlin. There, they began a dictionary of the German language that was to include words from three centuries. They died before it was completed, but the work was finished by their successors.

The world remains grateful to the Brothers Grimm for the vast treasury of stories they recorded.

Above: **Jacob (*right*) and Wilhelm Grimm were scholars whose studies of German folk literature produced a collection of popular fairy tales.**

Opposite: **Many German folk tales take place in the forest, including the popular story of "Little Red Riding Hood."**

Carnival

Carnival, or *Karneval* (KAHR-neh-vahl), is like the New Orleans Mardi Gras. In fact, it is a festival celebrated in many countries. It dates back to the Middle Ages when Christians indulged in a lot of merrymaking before Lent, a forty-day period of fasting and sacrifice leading up to Easter. However, some Carnival traditions have roots in pagan rituals. In ancient times, people dressed in frightening masks and costumes to scare away the rest of winter.

Theoretically, Carnival begins on November 11 at 11 a.m. — the eleventh hour on the eleventh day of the eleventh month. The real fun, however, does not start until late January or early February and the last few weeks leading up to Fastnacht Tuesday, the last day of Carnival. During this time, people dress up in

Left: **Children also dress up for Carnival. A Children's Carnival is held on the last Saturday or Sunday of the festival.**

costumes and paint their faces. It is like Halloween spread out over three long weekends. Adults participate with as much enthusiasm as children.

Celebrations really get into gear on the last weekend before Lent. People fill the streets, restaurants, bars, and clubs that are decorated with banners, flags, balloons, and streamers. In many cities, there are big parades with elaborate floats with people on board who throw candy and small medallions into the huge crowds. Most of the events are organized by Carnival clubs, whose members spend an entire year preparing for just this one festival.

There are special parades and parties for children. Typically, Children's Carnival takes place on the last Saturday or Sunday before Lent. Most of the events are scheduled in the afternoon so that even the youngest of children can participate.

One of the high points of the Carnival celebration is Women's Carnival, which falls on the last Thursday before Lent. On that day, women are supposed to be the bosses everywhere. In cities such as Cologne, Düsseldorf, and Mainz, it is a tradition for women to cut off mens' ties. Men in those areas have learned to wear ties they are not particularly fond of.

Above: Carnival celebrations differ from place to place. However, one thing they all have in common is that people wear masks and fun costumes.

49

Castles

Choose just about any part of the country, and you can spend a whole day visiting one castle after another.

Why does Germany have so many castles? The answer is that Germany did not become a unified country until 1871. Until then, it was a patchwork of feudal states. Some states, such as Prussia, Saxony, and Bavaria, were large, but most others were small. Their rulers had royal titles, but they did not wield much power. Most of the small states pledged their allegiance to more mighty sovereigns, who in turn gave them support and protection.

Rulers of this era demonstrated their authority and prestige by building castles. Instead of one or two castles, they built several. The powerful kings of Prussia, Saxony, Bavaria, and Württemberg maintained a number of castles in different parts of their kingdoms. This allowed the kings to establish a presence throughout their realm and gave them various places to go for a change of scenery. In addition, it was common for the ruler of a small state to pledge loyalty to a larger state in exchange for money to build a new castle.

Opposite: **Neuschwanstein Castle in Bavaria. King Louis II's desire for castles bankrupted Bavaria. In 1886, the king, also called Mad King Ludwig, was declared insane and removed to Berg Castle, where he was later found drowned in the nearby lake.**

Left: **Linderhof Palace. When he became king of Bavaria in 1864, Louis II was eighteen years old. It soon became clear that he was not suited to be a ruler. However, he built some magnificent castles. Linderhof Palace is a reflection of his artistic and fanciful personality.**

Dying Forests

Ancient Germanic pagan rituals included the worship of trees. People once believed that the gods made their earthly homes in trees. Indeed, chopping down sacred trees was considered a major crime.

Even though the pagan religions died out many centuries ago, the descendants of these people still hold a great affection for their beautiful forests. There is almost a mystical attachment between Germans and their forests. Just think of the fairy tales of the Brothers Grimm and of how many take place in the forest.

Nevertheless, today's Germans confront a disturbing phenomenon called *Waldsterben* (VALT-shtair-ben), or "dying forest." It is not a new problem. Periodic outbreaks of tree-killing diseases have been observed over the last 250 years. In 1883, the Germans prepared a map of damaged forests and found that areas near heavy industry were the most affected.

In the 1970s, a new kind of damage was observed, covering wide areas, often far from industrial sectors. Symptoms are a thinning of the tree tops, and needles and leaves turning yellow or white. Some of Germany's most beloved spots are affected, including the Bavarian Forest, the Bavarian Alps, and the Black Forest.

Above: **Germans have always had a special attachment to their forests. The Black Forest has been a popular hiking spot since the eighteenth century.**

In response to Waldsterben, substantial controls on emissions and pollution were put in place during the 1970s. However, a 1992 study by the federal government indicated that the problem had grown worse. A prime cause seems to be the large amount of air pollution from the eastern part of the country and Eastern European countries.

Reduction of emissions from road traffic, industry, and energy production are some of the measures taken to reduce air pollution. Foresters try to control damage, but their steps alone cannot solve the problem. In the meantime, more and more of Germany's beloved forests are dying, and Germans are asking themselves if they are doing enough to stop it.

AIR POLLUTION

Today, more than two-thirds of all forest trees in Germany are either damaged or weakened, making them more susceptible to secondary pests. Many conifers have been affected, but beech and oak trees have also been hit hard. Air pollution from factories, car emissions, and acid rain are blamed.

Left: Yellow or white leaves and the thinning of tree tops are symptoms of a dying forest. Substantial pollution controls and advances in forestry management help combat this phenomenon.

Government Funding of the Arts

Germany has a long tradition of government funding of the arts. Artists once used to depend on financial support from royal courts. Today, this support comes from democratically elected governments. In fact, Germany distributes more money per capita to cultural projects than any other country in the world. In a country with a population of eighty-two million, about thirty billion Deutsche marks are given to the arts.

The money comes from federal, state, and local governments and is distributed in different forms. Some funds go directly to the artists so they can support themselves. Government subsidies also go to theaters, galleries, museums, and art institutions. Block grants are distributed each year, and the recipients decide how to spend the money.

So what does all this **money buy?** Some people dispute the quality of the art produced by government funding. Others

Below: Berlin's Pergamon Museum contains one of the seven wonders of the world, the Pergamon Altar (180–159 B.C.) from Western Turkey.

Left: **In Germany, art is on display everywhere, including public spaces. This sculpture is in the center of Berlin.**

believe that, for the most part, the money is well spent and the majority of the art produced is worthwhile. However, there is a running joke in Germany — when people see a boring film, an odd theater production, or a questionable painting or sculpture, they say, "It must have been made with government arts promotion funds."

Still, very few people question the idea of arts being funded by the government. They may get irritated occasionally, but most people accept the principle that some tax money should go to deserving arts groups and projects. When citizens sit enraptured by one of Germany's celebrated symphony orchestras, delight in the precision of a premier ballet troupe, or view a large exhibition by a great painter or group of painters, they realize that these displays of art would not have been possible without government support.

Kindergartens

Kindergarten is a German word that means "children's garden." Both the name and the institution were created by Friedrich Wilhelm Fröbel, a German educator and social philosopher who believed that exposing young children to new sensory experiences, art forms, and nature would help their intellectual and emotional development. In 1837, he opened the world's first kindergarten for children ages three to six. Since then, kindergartens have spread around the world and developed in many different forms.

In Germany, the kindergarten remains an important institution. Roughly 50 percent of the paid work in Germany is done by women. Their contribution is vital to the economy. If they are to work, however, they need good child care. In order to help women build careers and also have children, the German federal government passed a law in 1996 that guarantees a place in kindergarten for every child.

Some are privately run, and others are funded by the state and churches. Kindergartens run for half-day sessions in the

Below: Child care is a big consideration for working mothers. In Germany, every child is guaranteed a place in kindergarten.

Left: **In kindergarten, children learn to get along with others and are exposed to new sensory experiences.**

mornings or afternoons, or for the entire day. Working parents typically drop their children off after 7:30 a.m. and pick them up on their way home from work at 5 p.m. Many kindergartens do not provide lunch. Children must be picked up at lunch time and brought back in the early afternoon.

People who study population trends are concerned about Germany's low birth rate. To encourage the birth rate, new parents in Germany are granted special leave for raising children. Up to three years of time off (in total, for both parents) from their job is guaranteed so they can be with their child. How they divide the time between them is up to the parents. For example, the mother could take the first year and the father the next two years. The parent who stays at home receives a government subsidy.

Learning a Trade

In North America, if you want to open a bakery, all you need to do is rent a storefront, get the necessary equipment and licenses, and then sell your wares to the public. Your success will depend on whether people like your products or not.

Above: **Young people learn trades such as welding by working under the supervision of a master craftsman.**

Guilds and Apprentices

In Germany, it is not that easy to set up a bakery. As in any other trade, you are required to go through a training program. Only when you complete the program and receive your *Meisterbrief* (MY-stair-breef), or master's certificate, can you begin to practice your trade. This master's certificate is also required for plumbing, carpentry, electrical work, housepainting, hairstyling, masonry, chimney-sweeping, and other skilled occupations.

All skilled trades are organized into guilds. Guild members possess the Meisterbrief and are responsible for teaching apprentices who want to learn their particular trade. This organization of craftspeople into guilds started in the twelfth century.

An average apprenticeship runs three years, although, depending on the trade, it can vary from two to three-and-a-half years. After learning the basics, apprentices are allowed to work under the supervision of a craftsperson who possesses the Meisterbrief and is thus qualified to train. They also spend part of the week attending theoretical courses in a vocational school. As they learn more and their skills improve, apprentices' salaries increase. However, they do not get as much as a fully-trained master even though they often do a lot of the work.

Becoming a Master

At the end of the training period, there is an examination administered by the local *Handwerkskammer* (HAHND-vairks-kahm-murr), or Chamber of Craft Guilds. Those who pass receive the *Gesellenbrief* (guh-ZELL-en-breef) certificate. A further five years of working and night classes are usually necessary to receive the Meisterbrief. With this master's certificate, crafts-people can work at full pay in the firm that trained them, go to another firm, or start their own business.

Below: Brewing good beers is an ancient art in Germany. Learning the skill, as with many other trades, first requires spending time as an apprentice.

The Max Planck Society

Leading the World in Science

One of the world's great scientific organizations is the Max Planck Society for the Promotion of Science. It was founded in 1911 at a time when German scientists led the world in scientific achievement. The society was initially named after the German Kaiser, William I. Then, in 1948, it was reorganized and renamed after the brilliant scientist, Max Planck, who won the Nobel Prize for Physics in 1918.

The society is an umbrella organization of many scientific institutes. It receives government support as well as grants from the private sector. There are three main research sections — the Biological-Medical Section, the Chemical-Physical-Technical Section, and the Arts and Humanities Section. There are at least eleven other related institutes. All of the institutes do research in their respective fields with their own scientists and outside specialists. They work closely with scientific groups around the world. In fact, it was a series

Below: **Professor Christiane Nuesslein-Volhard is a director of the Max Planck Institute in Tübingen. She is the first German woman to win a Nobel Prize.**

Left: Synthesis of plastics at a lab in the Max Planck Institute for Polymer Research in Mainz. Scientists associated with the Max Planck institutes have been at the forefront of scientific research since the early 1900s.

of projects with Max Planck Society institutes and Israel's renowned Weizmann Institute in the late 1950s that laid the groundwork for diplomatic relations between Israel and Germany. Until then, Israel was reluctant to have anything to do with Germany because of the persecution of the Jews during the Nazi era.

"Super Noses" and More

One of the society's most interesting accomplishments is the "super nose," an Alpha Proton X Ray Spectrometer that was developed by the Max Planck Institute for Chemistry in Mainz. It was used by the *Sojourner* rover on the planet Mars. The super nose can quickly determine a rock's composition by analyzing the spray of alpha particles, protons, and X rays coming from the rock. Ten years of research went into developing it.

The Oberammergau Passion Play

One of the world's most famous and longest-running amateur theater spectacles takes place every ten years in Oberammergau, a small town in the mountains of southern Germany. The play's roots are traced to a miracle believed to have occurred in Oberammergau in the seventeenth century.

In 1633, the people of Germany experienced a terrible outbreak of the plague. The townspeople of Oberammergau vowed that if God saved them from the disease, they would produce a play every ten years reenacting the passion, death, and resurrection of Jesus Christ. After the vow was made, the

Left: **When the Passion Plays are performed, Oberammergau is transformed from a small town into a theater center with visitors from around the world. These houses with frescoes painted on the outside walls are typical of homes in southern Bavaria.**

plague continued to ravage the rest of the country but spared Oberammergau. Some said it was a miracle. In 1634, the people of Oberammergau kept their promise, and the Passion Play was performed for the first time.

In keeping with the vow, the play is still performed by the townspeople every ten years. The cast includes hundreds of people of all age groups, giving everyone a chance to participate. The play runs from May to September, and each performance lasts two days with breaks for lunch and intermissions. The entire play is in four parts, with seventeen acts and many scene and set changes.

When the play was first performed, it was only for people in the area. Now visitors come from all over the world. The auditorium has a seating capacity of 4,800 and overlooks the world's largest open-air stage. The play is performed in years

Below: **The Passion Play reenacts Christ's death and resurrection. Hundreds of people participate, including children and senior citizens. People with regular jobs become actors as the time for the next production approaches.**

ending with zero and for special occasions. Over the years, the story has undergone changes. It now tells the story of the Old and New Testaments starting with the Fall of Adam and Eve in the Garden of Eden and runs all the way to the resurrection of Christ. In 1970, the text was changed in response to the Catholic Church's ruling that it was wrong to blame Jews for the death of Christ. In the year 2000, non-Christian residents of Oberammergau will be allowed to perform for the first time.

Private Gardens

Germans have the largest number of gardens in the world, but walking through a city or town, you might wonder where these gardens are. They are kept in special areas known as *Schrebergarten* (SHRAY-bair-GARR-ten) colonies.

The name comes from Daniel Gottlob Moritz Schreber, a German doctor who lived from 1808 to 1861. A native of Leipzig, he was a specialist in orthopedics and curative gymnastics. Industrialization was just beginning, and Dr. Schreber was very interested in the health of the working class. For example, he stressed the importance of playgrounds for children. Although not much of a gardener himself, Schreber founded the movement

Left: **Gardening is an activity for people of all ages. Tens of thousands of small enclosed gardens, such as this one, exist today throughout Germany.**

Above: **Sheds in the gardens are used for storage. Some are quite attractive and decorated with personal touches, such as the owner's coat of arms.**

for these small gardens as a way to get poor people out of unhealthy environments and in contact with nature.

The idea spread rapidly throughout Germany. It reached its peak in the 1950s when increasing affluence and leisure time allowed more people to acquire a Schrebergarten, a small garden of their own. Today, there are tens of thousands of these small, enclosed plots throughout Germany. Many of them have little sheds built on them.

From the first signs of spring through the last chilly days of autumn, people tend their gardens. Schrebergarten colonies are usually organized and administered by clubs. The clubs set the rules, often determining what can be grown and the size and appearance of individual gardens. Owners of a neglected garden plot, for example, might be warned that they are hurting club morale.

Many people do not grow anything special in their Schrebergarten. For them, the gardens are places where they can get away from the stresses of daily urban life. In this respect, the gardens can be seen as miniature country retreats at the edge of a city or town.

Recycling

After decades of heavy and uncontrolled industrialization, Germans are now very aware of the environment and how damaging industrial waste can be. They also live in a small country with a fairly large population and few natural resources. So the Germans have developed one of the most advanced recycling systems in the world.

Green Dots?

The most popular and effective system is the *Grüner Punkt* (GROON-urr POONKT), or "Green Dot," system introduced in 1993. It is based on an agreement between German state governments and a private nonprofit organization, Grüner Punkt. Many products in shops carry the Grüner Punkt symbol, a green dot with two swirling arrows.

Grüner Punkt provides businesses and households with special trash containers marked with their green dot stickers. The trash is then collected, processed, and recycled.

Below: Germans are concerned about their environment and have several recycling programs. Paper, glass, cardboard, plastic, tin, and alloyed metals are all recycled. Containers for sorting trash for recycling are a common sight.

Left: **Everyone, including private citizens, is encouraged to recycle their trash.**

Green Shopping

Support for this recycling effort also comes from German manufacturers and consumers. Buyers look for the green dot symbol on their purchases because it means the packaging can be placed into a Grüner Punkt trash bin and recycled.

Of course, Grüner Punkt does not do all this work for free. The manufacturers must pay a fee to use the green dot symbol and to have their products and packaging collected and recycled. You might think it would be cheaper for manufacturers not to use the Grüner Punkt system, but just the opposite is true. The majority of German shoppers are environmentally conscious and therefore, prefer products with the Grüner Punkt symbol even if they cost a bit more. They gladly buy the green dot products, feeling content that they are doing their part to protect the environment when they shop. The success of this program is a sign of Germans' increasing concern for the environment.

Superhighways

Speed Unlimited

The *Autobahn* (AW-to-bahn) is a highway system stretching over 6,800 miles (11,000 km) throughout Germany. It was started by the Nazi government in the 1930s as a public works project to provide much-needed employment and a transportation network for military vehicles. The Autobahn survived the Nazis and is now a symbol of the prosperity of post-war Germany.

The Autobahn has long enjoyed a reputation for being a motorway with no posted speed limits. Rumor has it that drivers can drive as fast as their cars will go. Since German cars are famous for their high performance and speed, it is not unusual to see cars reaching speeds of 120 miles (193 km) per hour. German drivers applaud this free-throttle policy, as they race along at frightening speeds. Some foreign drivers look forward to visiting Germany, where they can rent a fast car and enjoy the experience of driving at high speeds.

During peak holidays, however, even the Autobahn gets badly jammed with traffic, and people may spend hours sitting in traffic. Different states, therefore, try to stagger holidays.

Above: **Germany's Autobahn attracts motorists who like to drive at high speeds, as well as those who enjoy beautiful scenery. There are rest stops about every 30 miles (48 km).**

Restrictions

Unlimited speeding on the Autobahn is actually more legend than fact. Restrictions are posted allowing unlimited speeding only under certain weather and traffic conditions. For instance, if it is raining or snowing, speed limits must be observed. There are also slow-down zones, where drivers are required to reduce their speed to 60 miles (96 km) per hour.

Dangers of the Road

Sadly, many people do not observe these restrictions and keep driving at inappropriate speeds. As a result, Germany has one of the highest highway accident death rates in the world. A large number of people now argue that the government should establish a maximum speed limit. There are also those who believe speed limits should be set in order to control the pollution now destroying Germany's forests.

Politicians are not eager to take what would probably be a very unpopular step, and it is unlikely that a speed limit will be set for the entire Autobahn. Despite the high number of highway fatalities and the pollution caused by speeding cars, many Germans do not want to give up the pleasure of traveling on the road as fast as their cars will take them.

Below: **Originally designed as a network of roads for military vehicles, the Autobahn is now one of the most efficient highway systems in the world.**

Techno Music

The Nazis fought diligently against the influence of American culture. Jazz, for example, was deemed "unacceptable." However, after World War II, American music became very popular. German music, on the other hand, made little impact beyond the borders of the German-speaking world.

Over the last ten years, all that has changed. The worldwide explosion of techno music has put Germany at the forefront of international pop music. Techno music is electronic music created by mixing synthesized sounds and setting them to a strong beat that is perfect for dancing. While many people love the music, others hate it. The heavy, repetitive beat is hypnotic. Those who like it say the music allows them to fall into a meditative, trance-like state as they listen and dance. But others simply find it boring and annoying.

Unlike most musical forms, techno music actually has no performing artists or recording stars. The creators of techno songs

Below: Techno music lovers enjoy dancing to synthesized sounds set to a strong beat.

are the disc jockeys who mix various sounds "live" at techno discos or in recording studios. Some of this mixing is done randomly, and some of it is planned.

The origins of techno music can be traced to a German recording group, *Kraftwerk* (KRAHFT-vairk), that started experimenting in the 1970s with synthesized sound and repetitive musical lines. The trend was further developed in the 1980s in places outside Germany, such as Chicago, Illinois and Detroit, Michigan. However, since Germany is where the music started, it is still considered the techno music center. German DJs such as Talla 2xlc or Sven Väth travel to other parts of the world to host techno music concerts called "raves." This type of German pop music does not have a language barrier because few words are used.

The big event for techno music lovers is the annual Love Parade in Berlin. Every summer, thousands of techno fans gather from all over the world to dance along a huge avenue in the center of town where the Kaiser's armies once marched. For an entire weekend, this avenue, surrounded by a park, is closed to regular traffic to make room for a parade of floats and crowds of techno music fans.

Above: **Berlin's Love Parade is an annual event that attracts techno music lovers from around the world.**

Women in Government

Few and Far Between

Over the past fifteen years, more and more women have become politically active and part of the government. They are challenging a long-standing German tradition of "men only" in political offices.

The first attempts at German democracy were dominated by men. The tradition continued with the founding of the Federal Republic of Germany in 1949. Although all adult German citizens had the right to vote, the very first Bundestag had only 6.8 percent female representation, and all those women held minor positions. The worst representation for women came in the 1972–1976 Bundestag when it hit a low of 5.8 percent. The irony is that this Bundestag was considered very progressive and one that sought to correct social injustices.

Many women decided they needed to be more politically involved and start pushing for better representation in the Parliament. The number of women in the Bundestag slowly grew over the years. By 1994, 26.3 percent of the seats were held by women. The major political parties have established female quotas for the party committees, which make many important decisions.

Below: **Most representatives to the German Parliament, or Bundestag, are men. However, more women are joining the government at local, state, and federal levels.**

Moving into Positions of Power

Just having more members in the parliament is not enough, however. Women have also been working to get into positions of greater power. There was no woman in a full cabinet position until Elizabeth Schwarzhaupt became Minister of Health in 1961. This health ministry, which also added responsibility for family and youth matters, then became known as the "woman's cabinet post." But women were not trusted with any further cabinet responsibilities until the talented Marie Schlei held the post of Minister of Economic Cooperation in the late 1970s. There was finally a big advance for women in the 1987–1990 Parliament, when seven out of thirty-five cabinet members were women. But to this day, no woman has been seriously considered for the top post of chancellor.

There have also been few opportunities for women at the local level. Heidi Simonis, the governor of Schleswig-Holstein, is the country's only female governor. Frankfurt's mayor, Petra Roth, is the first woman mayor of a major German city. Many people feel that women have to gain more power at the local level before they can achieve the top posts with greater power. Most observers of German politics agree.

Above, left: **Professor Dr. Rita Süssmuth was the Minister for Youth, Family, and Health from 1985 to 1988. She was made Bundestag president in 1988. She is the first woman to hold the post.**

Above, right: **Antje Vollmer has served in the Bundestag since she was elected as a Green Party candidate in 1983. She, along with her party, has helped pass important environmental legislation.**

RELATIONS WITH NORTH AMERICA

A longstanding friendship exists between Germany and North America. It began during the American Revolution and was nurtured by German immigrants who came to the New World in search of better opportunities. Their contributions to their new homeland included hard work, expertise, and a love of German culture. Today, the people and leaders of Germany, the United States, and Canada share an appreciation for each other's traditions. They work together at many levels.

Opposite: **German Hessian Hussars were hired by the British to fight the American rebels during the American Revolution. But they joined forces with the colonists instead and later became citizens of the newly independent United States.**

When World War I broke out in 1914, the U.S. leaders faced a dilemma. Britain and France, united against Germany, were seen as offering a better chance for promoting democratic values and American business interests in Europe. However, with so many Americans claiming German heritage, the United States faced a difficult decision. For the next three years, therefore, a propaganda campaign was waged in the United States. Germany was portrayed in a negative light, especially in Hollywood films.

Above: **U.S. President Bill Clinton and German Chancellor Dr. Helmut Kohl met in Milwaukee, Wisconsin, in 1996 to discuss issues important to both their countries.**

Enemies

In 1915, a German war submarine sank the *Lusitania*, a British passenger ship. Twelve hundred passengers drowned, including 128 Americans. The sinking became a rallying point for action against Germany. Finally, in 1917, a telegram from Germany's Under-Secretary of State for Foreign Affairs, Arthur Zimmerman, urging Mexico and Japan to attack the United States, was too much.

The United States entered World War I against Germany and its allies on April 16, 1917. This tipped the balance against Germany and its smaller, weaker allies. They surrendered on November 11, 1918. The Kaiser abdicated and went into exile. Democratic forces formed the country's first popularly elected government, the Weimar Republic.

Relations between North America and the new Weimar Republic were cordial. However, the bond was not developed because, after World War I, the United States and Canada adopted a policy of isolationism and turned their attentions inward.

By the time the ultra-right wing National Socialist Party, or Nazis, came to power in 1933, Franklin D. Roosevelt had been elected president of the United States. The contrasts in style and social philosophy between the two governments led to a cooling of diplomatic relations that developed into a deep freeze with the outbreak of World War II.

Left: **After World War II, West Berlin was occupied by troops from the United States, Great Britain, and France.**

Left: **After World War II, Americans helped their former German enemies by sending them packages of food and daily essentials during their occupation of Germany. An enduring friendship was established that continues to this day.**

Although officially neutral for the first two years of World War II, the United States once more supported Great Britain and France, this time with money and arms. This angered the Nazis, and four days after the Japanese bombed Pearl Harbor, Germany declared war on the United States.

World War II ended with a total and devastating defeat for Germany. The victors — the United States, Great Britain, France, and the Soviet Union — divided Germany, each taking a sector. This brought about a strange transformation in relations between Germany and the United States. Before the war, the United States was closer to its ally, the U.S.S.R. During the occupation, however, the United States developed stronger ties with Germany.

Renewed Friendship

Germans also became more open to Americans. Having lived through the horrors of the Nazi dictatorship, many Germans wanted to cast off the past and build a new, democratic Germany. Those in the U.S. occupied zone were attracted to the American way of life. They were also grateful for the food and material goods the Americans provided. In turn, North American leaders saw Germany as an ally in the fight against communism.

Below: **Friendship between the two countries reached its peak in 1963 when President John F. Kennedy visited West Berlin. He declared continuing American support for the divided city by ending his speech with the ringing phrase, *"Ich bin ein Berliner"* (I am a Berliner).**

77

Mixed Relations

In 1949, the three zones occupied by the Americans, French, and British combined to form the Federal Republic of Germany, popularly referred to as West Germany. The United States was its staunchest supporter. The Cold War and fear of military aggression from nearby communist countries bound the U.S. and Germany closer together with military alliances. In 1955, Germany joined the North Atlantic Treaty Organization (NATO).

Actions and policies of the United States during the Vietnam War, however, disturbed many West Germans, and resulted in demonstrations at U.S. military bases. Friction between the two countries arose again in the early 1980s when the American arms race with the Soviet Union intensified. The United States stationed more weapons, including nuclear warheads, in Germany. Relations with communist East Germany followed the party line of the U.S.S.R. Officially, the United States was seen as an archenemy.

Since 1990, there has been a united Germany. German friendship with North America remains. However, Germans are now paying more attention to strengthening their European ties.

Below: **In the early 1980s, Germans worried about the buildup of U.S. troops and nuclear weapons. To show their displeasure, they held public demonstrations such as this one in Frankfurt.**

Left: **Entertainer Ron Williams is one of many Americans who have found a niche in Germany.**

North American Presence in Germany

After World War II, thousands of U.S. troops and civilians in support services were stationed in Germany, along with a small contingent of Canadians. Since 1990, the number of troops has been cut drastically. Most of the remaining North Americans work for multinational companies that were sent to Germany by their home offices. However, there are also those who came on their own, filling important gaps in the employment market.

American Artists in Germany

Some Americans have established successful careers in the entertainment industry in Germany. For instance, Ron Williams, a former GI, is now a German television celebrity. North Americans have also excelled in the arts. One of Germany's most famous choreographers is a New York native — William Forsythe of the Frankfurt Ballet.

German Immigration to North America

While only 4.7 percent of the Canadian population claims German ancestry, more Americans claim German blood than any other ancestry. Religious refugees formed the first large wave of German immigrants to North America in the eighteenth century. Most of them were members of religious minorities, such as the Mennonites and the Amish. There are large communities of them today in Ontario, Canada and in the central United States.

During the American Revolution, the British sent German troops to fight the American rebels. These soldiers were from Hesse and were known as fierce fighters. But when the German troops arrived in the New World, the colonists told them of their

cause and offered them land if they switched sides. They did, and after the war, these Germans became farmers and citizens of the new nation. Another German who helped the American cause was Baron von Steuben, a Prussian general and brilliant military strategist who helped defeat the British.

A second and much larger wave of immigration took place in the nineteenth century with the arrival of close to seven million Germans. Most of them came for better economic opportunities.

Above: **Amish communities in the United States still follow the religious principles of their homeland. Their German ancestors emigrated in the eighteenth century to escape religious persecution.**

Despite Germany's growing industrialization, there was still great poverty in cities and on farms. Farmers often tilled the land for large estate owners and earned little in return. They were attracted by North America's vast farmlands. Many of them settled in the American Midwest and Canadian prairie regions.

These immigrants are remembered for their contributions to America's economic growth and success. The Heinz family of Germany settled in Pittsburgh in 1869 and founded what is today a global food empire that includes the all-American favorite, Heinz ketchup. Blue jeans were the idea of Levi Strauss, a German from Bavaria who developed a sturdy pair of pants for work and play.

Left: **Baron von Steuben was a Prussian general who fought on the side of the Americans during the American Revolution. His brilliant military strategies helped defeat the British.**

Left: The largest wave of German immigrants was in the early 1900s. They traveled by boat in crowded and cramped conditions because many of them were poor.

Below: Henry Kissinger was born in Germany in 1923 and came to the United States with his parents when he was a child to escape Nazi persecution. As Secretary of State for U.S. presidents Richard Nixon and Gerald Ford, Kissinger was an influential figure in American foreign policy.

Searching for Political Freedom

The third wave of German immigration in the nineteenth and early twentieth centuries included people in search of political freedom. Many of these immigrants were young men who came to avoid being drafted into the German army. Ironically, some of these same men fought valiantly in the American Civil War when they thought the cause was just. One immigrant who came in search of human rights was Carl Schurz, founder of the American Federation of Labor (AFL), which later joined with the Congress of Industrial Organizations (CIO) to become the AFL-CIO.

In the 1930s, there was yet another wave of German immigration, smaller than the previous ones, but still very significant. These new immigrants were refugees from Nazi persecution. With their knowledge and talent, they made great contributions to their adopted homeland.

One of the best known is Albert Einstein, a Nobel Prize-winning physicist and creator of the Theory of Relativity. Thomas Mann, considered the greatest German writer of his day and winner of the 1929 Nobel Prize for Literature, went with his wife, Elizabeth, to southern California. Many famous filmmakers and leading German actors also fled Nazi Germany and established careers in Hollywood, despite the language problem. Marlene Dietrich, for example, was an extremely popular actress and singer in both her native Germany and America.

German immigration to North America has not stopped. Contemporary immigrants typically come because Canada and the United States are still seen as lands of great opportunity, where innovation and creativity are encouraged and rewarded. However, today's new arrivals come because they choose to and not because they are being driven from their homeland by poverty or persecution.

Above, left: Nobel Prize-winning author Thomas Mann fled Germany when Hitler came to power in 1933. Mann and his wife, Elizabeth, fled first to Switzerland and then the United States. He became a U.S. citizen in 1944.

Above, right: Famous for his Theory of Relativity, German scientist Albert Einstein won the Nobel Prize for Physics in 1921. In 1933, he joined the Institute for Advanced Study in Princeton, New Jersey. He became a U.S. citizen in 1940. Einstein was one of the scientists who helped develop the atomic bomb.

Cultural Connections and Influences

What would America be without the frankfurter and the hamburger? As their names suggest, these two popular foods originated in the German cities of Frankfurt and Hamburg.

However, many German customs have had an even greater influence on North American culture. The Christmas tree with its bright decorations came from Germany. Many famous Christmas songs, such as "Silent Night" ("Stille Nacht") and "O Christmas Tree" ("O Tannenbaum"), were originally written in the German language.

Some cultural influences are the result of a strong trading relationship. Probably the best examples of successful German exports to North America are cars. The Mercedes-Benz, BMW, Volkswagen, Porsche, and Audi are all triumphs of German engineering and marketing. But how many people are aware that Bayer aspirin is also a German product, made by the huge Bayer pharmaceutical company of Leverkusen?

Of course, these cultural influences have not been only one-way. American influence in Germany over the last fifty years has been extensive, especially in music and cinema. Many of Germany's top ten movies and songs are American-made.

Opposite: **One of the best-known manufacturers of high-performance cars is Mercedes-Benz. These 1996 models are on display at a car show in Berlin. The Kaiser Wilhelm Memorial Church, built in 1895, is in the background.**

Below: **This office building and museum in Munich belongs to the German car manufacturer, Bayerische Motoren Werke, better known as BMW.**

GERMANY

N

SWEDEN

DENMARK

BALTIC SEA

NORTH SEA

● Kiel

SCHLESWIG-HOLSTEIN

MECKLENBURG-WESTERN POMERANIA

POLAND

● Hamburg

Elbe

Oder

● Bremen

Weser

LOWER SAXONY

■ BERLIN

● Hannover

BRANDENBURG

THE NETHERLANDS

● Hameln

● Magdeburg

SAXONY-ANHALT

● Wittenberg

NORTH RHINE-WESTPHALIA

HARZ MTS

Saale

Elbe

● Leipzig

Ruhr Industrial Area

● Dortmund

● Düsseldorf

SAXONY

BELGIUM

● Cologne

● Bonn

THURINGIA

● Dresden

Rhine

HESSE

RHINELAND-PALATINATE

TAUNUS MTS.

● Frankfurt

● Hanau

Main

CZECH REPUBLIC

● Mainz

● Mannheim

LUXEMBOURG

SAARLAND

● Heidelberg

● Nuremberg (Nürnberg)

Bohemian Forest

Bavarian Forest

● Karlsruhe

BAVARIA

Rhine

Black Forest

● Stuttgart

● Tübingen

Danube

FRANCE

BADEN-WÜRTTEMBERG

● Munich

AUSTRIA

Lake Constance

● Oberammergau

BERCHTESGADEN ALPS

BAVARIAN ALPS

Zugspitze (9,718 feet/2,962 m)

	International Boundary
	State Boundary
■	Capital
●	City
∿	River

SWITZERLAND

ITALY

86

Above: Street musicians entertain passersby in the old city of Frankfurt.

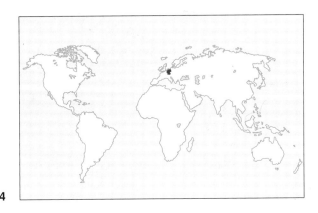

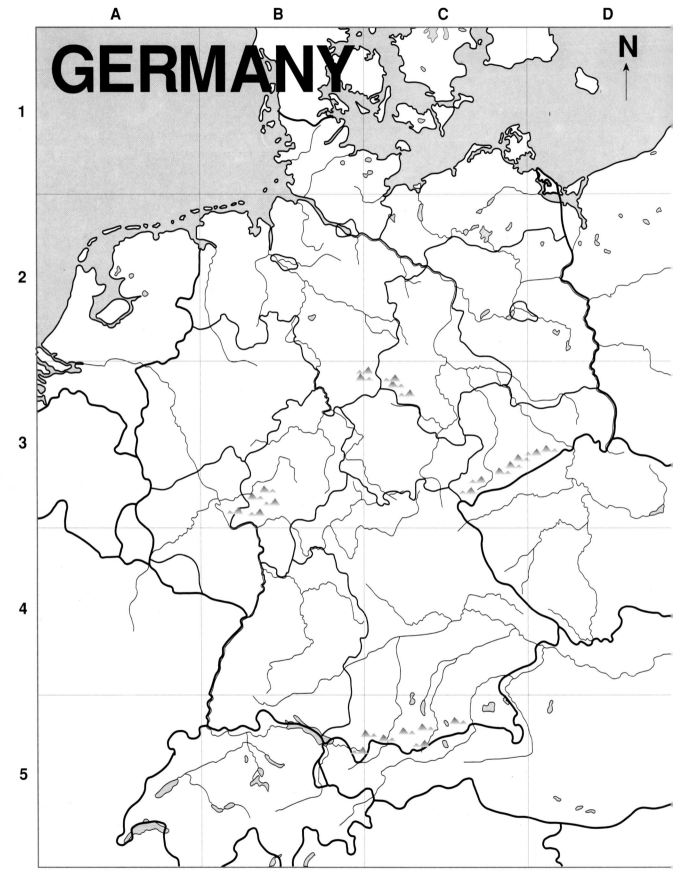

GERMANY

N

How Is Your Geography?

Learning to identify the main geographical areas and points of a country can be challenging. Although it may seem difficult at first to memorize the location and spelling of major cities or the names of mountain ranges, rivers, deserts, lakes, and other prominent physical features, the end result of this effort can be very rewarding. Places you previously did not know existed will suddenly come to life when referred to in world news, whether in newspapers, television reports, or other books and reference sources. This knowledge will make you feel a bit closer to the rest of the world, with its fascinating variety of cultures and physical geography.

Used in a classroom setting, the instructor can make duplicates of this map using a copy machine (PLEASE DO NOT WRITE IN THIS BOOK!). Students can then fill in any requested information on their individual map copies. Used one-on-one, the student can also make copies of the map on a copy machine and use them as a study tool. The student can practice identifying place names and geographical features on his or her own.

Above: **Heidelberg is a medieval city famous for its beautiful scenery and castle ruins.**

Germany at a Glance

Official Name   Bundesrepublik Deutschland, Federal Republic of Germany

Capital   Berlin

Seat of Government   Bonn

Official Language   German

Population   82 million

Land Area   137,744 square miles (357,000 square kilometers)

States   Baden-Württemberg, Bavaria, Berlin, Brandenburg, Bremen, Hamburg, Hesse, Lower Saxony, Mecklenburg-Western Pomerania, North Rhine-Westphalia, Rhineland-Palatinate, Saarland, Saxony, Saxony-Anhalt, Schleswig-Holstein, Thuringia

Highest Point   Zugspitze (9,718 feet/2,962 meters)

Major Rivers   Rhine, Elbe, Main

Major Mountains   Bavarian Alps, Harz Mountains

Main Religions   Lutheran Church, Roman Catholic Church

Famous Leaders   Otto von Bismarck, Adolf Hitler, Konrad Adenauer, Erich Honecker, Willi Brandt, Helmut Schmidt, Helmut Kohl

Major Festivals   Carnival (Karneval)
Oktoberfest
Christmas

Important Anniversaries   October 3 (Day of German Unity)

National Anthem   "Das Deutschland Lied" (The Germany Song)

Largest Cities   Berlin (population: 3.5 million)
Hamburg (population: 1.7 million
Munich (population: 1.2 million)

Currency   Deutsche mark (DM 1.78 = U.S. $1 as of 1998)

Opposite: **Charlottenburg Palace in Berlin was once the summer residence of Prussian kings.**

Glossary

German Vocabulary

Abitur (ah-bee-TOOR): a series of tests Gymnasium students take when they finish their studies.

Auf Wiedersehen (owff VEE-dair-SAY-hen): "Good-bye."

Autobahn (AW-to-bahn): a network of highways stretching over 6,800 miles (11,000 km) throughout Germany.

Bundesrat (boon-des-RAHT): house of state legislators in the German Parliament.

Bundestag (boon-des-TAHG): a house in the German Parliament consisting of 672 elected representatives.

Dirndl (DURN-dil): a skirt worn by Bavarian women.

Führer (FYUR-er): leader.

Fussball (FOOS-ball): soccer.

Grüner Punkt (GROON-urr POONKT): Green Dot; refers to a recycling system that identifies recycled and recyclable products with a green dot label.

Guten Appetit (GOO-ten upp-eh-TEET): "Enjoy your meal."

Gymnasium (gim-NAH-zee-oom): a school that prepares students for university studies and executive positions in industry and commerce.

Hauptschule (HOWPT-shool-uh): school that prepares students for jobs in trade and industry.

Kaffee (kahf-FAY): coffee; refers to the fourth meal of the day that includes coffee and pastries, usually cakes.

Kaiser (KYE-zer): emperor.

Karneval (KAHR-neh-vahl): Carnival.

Kraftwerk (KRAHFT-vairk): "power plant." It is the name of a band of German musicians who developed techno music.

Kulturvolk (kool-TOOR-fulk): a people of culture.

Lederhose (LAY-dare-HOSE-uh): men's short leather pants worn in Bavaria.

Mein Kampf (MINE KAHMF): *My Struggle*, or *My Fight*, the title of Hitler's book outlining his beliefs, written in 1923.

Meisterbrief (MY-stair-breef): a master's certificate granted to a craftsperson who has trained as an apprentice and passed an examination.

Realschule (ray-AHL-shool-uh): a school that prepares students for mid-level positions in business and public service jobs.

Reich (RIKE): empire.

Schnitzel (SHNIT-tsuhl): a thin, breaded cutlet.

Schrebergarten (SHRAY-bair-GARR-ten): a small, private garden.

Vereine (fur-INE-nuh): clubs.

Waldsterben (VALT-shtair-ben): dying forests.

English Vocabulary

Allies: refers to the countries that joined forces against Germany in World War II: Great Britain, the United States, France, the Soviet Union, and others.

apprentice: someone who is learning a trade by working with a master craftsperson.

beleaguered: to have difficulties.

blockade: (v) to close off and prevent entry or exit.

chancellor: the leader in the German government.

communism: a political movement based on the ideas of Karl Marx, who believed that all property belongs to the common community or state.

concentration camps: guarded compounds, such as those established by the Nazis, for the confinement of political prisoners. An estimated six million people died, many of them Jews, in Nazi camps.

East Germany: refers to the German Democratic Republic.

Federal Republic of Germany: the country formed in 1949, with a democratically elected government, and commonly referred to as West Germany.

German Democratic Republic: the country founded in 1949 and commonly referred to as East Germany. It was under the domination of the U.S.S.R.

guilds: organizations of master craftspeople who are responsible for teaching apprentices their trade.

Holy Roman Emperor: this title was first given by the pope in Rome to Charlemagne in A.D. 800. The title of Holy Roman Emperor was borne by German kings until 1806. Their empire is often called the Holy Roman Empire, but is not related to the Roman empire of ancient times.

Iron Curtain: an 855-mile (1,375-km), fortified border built in 1953 as a barrier between communist Eastern bloc countries and the rest of Europe.

Nobel Prizes: awards given each year, from a fund established by Swedish philanthropist Alfred Nobel, for outstanding achievements in physics, chemistry, medicine or physiology, literature, and the promotion of peace.

plague: an epidemic disease that kills many.

Protestant Reformation: a movement that began in 1517 when Martin Luther, a German monk, challenged the powers of the Roman Catholic Church.

reunification: the coming back of something broken apart. After forty-one years of separation, East and West Germany officially reunified and became one country again on October 3, 1990.

sirocco: a warm wind that blows in from North Africa and the Mediterranean Sea and across Germany.

streaming: a selection process starting in fifth-grade in which students are placed in schools based on their academic abilities.

Theory of Relativity: an important theory in physics developed by Nobel Prize winner Albert Einstein.

Thirty Years' War: a war fueled by religious hatred that reduced the power of the Hapsburg monarchy and turned Germany into a collection of small, independent kingdoms.

Versailles Treaty: a document signed in 1918 that dictated the terms of Germany's defeat after World War I.

Weimar Republic: Germany's first democratically elected government, founded in 1919.

More Books to Read

Country Topics for Craft Projects: Germany. Ting Morris, Neil Morris, and Rachel Wright (Franklin Watts)

Flying Against the Wind. Ina Friedman (Lodgepole Press)

Germany and the Germans. Focus on series. Anita Ganeri (Gloucester Press)

Germany. Cultures of the World series. Barbara Fuller (Times Editions)

Germany. Festivals of the World series. Richard Lord (Gareth Stevens)

Germany. Modern Industrial World. Patrick Burke (Thomson Learning)

Germany Then and Now (International Affairs). William Spencer (Franklin Watts)

Germany: United Again (The Fall of Communism). Jeffrey B. Symyrkywicz (Dillon Press)

Germany. Women in Society series. Agnes Bohnen (Times Editions)

Videos

Fodor's Video: Germany. (a co-production of Fodor's Travel Publications, Inc. and International Video Network)

Germany for All Seasons. (Travelview International)

Germany: the Rhine and Mosel, Romantic Road and Bavaria. (Small World Productions)

Lyric Language: German/English. (Penton Overseas)

Web Sites

userpage.chemie.fu-berlin.de/adressen/brd.html

userpage.chemie.fu-berlin.de/adressen/brd-fact.html

ms.linf.fu-berlin.de/czo/time-project/history.html

www.odyssey.net/subscribers/scior/lvbbiog.html

www2.whirlpool.com/html/homelife/cookin/cookkrec.htm

Due to the dynamic nature of the Internet, some web sites stay current longer than others. To find additional web sites, use a reliable search engine with one or more of the following keywords to help you locate information on Germany. Keywords: *Beethoven, Berlin Wall, fairy tales, Germans, Germany, Adolf Hitler, Helmut Kohl, Munich, and World War II.*

Index